LIFE SCIENCE IN DEPTH

CELLS
AND
CELL FUNCTION

Sally Morgan

Heinemann Library
Chicago, Illinois

© 2006 Heinemann Library
a division of Reed Elsevier Inc.
Chicago, Illinois

Customer Service 888-454-2279
Visit our website at www.heinemannraintree.com

Designed by Richard Parker and Q2A Solutions
Illustrations by Q2A Solutions

Printed and bound by South China Printing Company

10 09 08 07 06
10 9 8 7 6 5 4 3 2 1

Library of Congress Cataloging-in-Publication Data
Morgan, Sally.
    Cells and cell function / Sally Morgan.
        p. cm. -- (Life science in-depth)
    Includes bibliographical references and index.
    ISBN 1-4034-7520-2 (library binding - hardcover) -- ISBN 1-4034-7528-8 (pbk.)
    1. Cells--Juvenile literature. 2. Cell physiology--Juvenile literature.
    I. Title. II. Series.
    QH582.5.M67 2005
    571.6--dc22
                                                          2005023564

Acknowledgments
The author and publishers are grateful to the following for permission to reproduce copyright material: Alamy pp. **9** (Bob Schuchman), **56** (Crispin Hughes); BBC p. **59**; Corbis pp. **14** (Neil Miller), **21**; Getty Images p. **5** (Bob Thomas); Oxford Scientific pp. **28**, **48**; Science Photo Library pp. **57** (Alfred Pasieka), **47** (Astrid & Hanns-Frieder Michler), **22** (Biology Media), **7** (BSIP/Sercomi), **54** (CNRI), **1**, **38** (David Scharf), **24** (Dr. Yorgos Nikas), **20**, **31** (J. C. Revy), **52** (Kent Wood), **25** (M. I. Walker), **51** (Rosenfield Images Ltd), **43** (Simon Fraser), **19**, **32**, **44**.

Cover photograph of a cell, reproduced with permission of Science Photo Library/David Mack.

Our thanks to Emma Leatherbarrow for her assistance in the preparation of this book.

Every effort has been made to contact copyright holders of any material reproduced in this book. Any omissions will be rectified in subsequent printings if notice is given to the publisher.

The paper used to print this book comes from sustainable resources.

Contents

Words printed in the text in bold, **like this**, are explained in the Glossary.

What Are Cells?

The cell is the basic building block of life. When you look at yourself in a mirror, you see trillions of cells all working together. The smallest **organisms**, such as **bacteria**, consist of just a single cell, but most animals, plants, and **fungi** are multicellular, which means they are made up of many cells.

LOTS OF DIFFERENT TYPES OF CELL

Not only is the human body made up of trillions of cells, but there are also about 200 different types of cell. Each type has a specific job or role to carry out in the body. Our muscles are made of muscle cells, our livers of liver cells, and there are even very specialized types of cells that make the enamel of our teeth or the clear **lenses** in our eyes. Usually the structure of these different types of cells is specially **adapted** to their function. Cells of the same type group together to form **tissues**, and tissues form **organs**.

LARGE AND SMALL

Some cells are large and can be seen with the eye. The largest cell is the unfertilized egg cell of the ostrich, which is a massive 6 inches (15 centimeters) long! This is unusual, since most cells are just a fraction of a millimeter in length and can only be seen with a microscope. The largest human cells are about the diameter of a human hair, but most are smaller—about one-tenth of the diameter of a human hair.

GROWING MORE

One of the characteristics of life is growth. Growth occurs when cells get larger and divide to form new cells. Human beings begin life as a single cell: a fertilized egg. This cell divides into two and then four, eight, sixteen, and so on.

The individual cells grow to a maximum size, and then they divide. As you grow, you get more cells. An adult therefore has more cells than a child.

This book looks at the many different types of cells that are found in animals and plants as well as in bacteria and **viruses**. It examines why most cells, whether from an elephant or an earthworm, are microscopic in size. It also answers questions such as: Why don't cells grow larger and larger to become giant cells? How can a cell divide to form two new cells? This book also covers some of the issues relating to cells today, such as **cloning** and **genetic engineering**.

The size of cells does not vary between people. A large person does not have larger cells than a smaller person, but rather more of them.

Inside a Cell

Most cells are so small that they cannot be seen by the human eye. The only way to study them is to look at them using a microscope. This way, they can be viewed hundreds, even thousands of times their normal size. There are two types of microscope: the light microscope and the **electron** microscope.

THE LIGHT MICROSCOPE

Microscopes work in a similar way to a magnifying glass. A magnifying glass uses a lens to **focus** the light reflecting off an object into a larger image. In a light microscope, there is an eyepiece lens and up to three objective lenses. The specimen is placed on the stage under one of the objective lenses. It is illuminated (lit up) by a light placed under the stage. The objective lens is either raised or lowered to focus on the specimen. When users look through the eyepiece, they see a magnified image of the specimen.

eyepiece lens

coarse focus

fine focus

objective lens

specimen

stage

light source

A light microscope has a lens in the eyepiece that usually magnifies the image by x10 and three objective lenses that magnify the specimen by either x4, x10, or x40 times, giving a maximum magnification of x400.

UNDERSTANDING UNITS

When using microscopes, it is important to remember that the size of the different structures is really small. This table may help you figure out just how small something is.

1 millimeter (mm) = 0.039 inch (in.)

1 micrometer (μm) = 0.000039 inch (in.)

1 nanometer (nm) = 0.000000039 inch (in.)

ELECTRON MICROSCOPES

Most light microscopes give a maximum magnification of 400 times. The best light microscopes can magnify something about 2,000 times its original size, but an electron microscope can magnify a specimen up to two million times, allowing scientists to see cells in incredible detail. Electron microscopes, as the name suggests, use electrons rather than light to see the specimen. There are two common types of electron microscopes: transmission and scanning. The transmission electron microscope works in much the same way as a light microscope. These microscopes are used to study the contents of cells. A scanning electron microscope produces a picture of the surface of the specimen. It is useful for looking at the surface of cells, for example. In both types of electron microscope, the image is displayed on a monitor.

nucleus ——

This image of an animal cell was taken using a transmission electron microscope. It is possible to see the tiny structures in the cells, such as the nucleus.

LOOKING AT CELLS

When a cell is viewed using a light microscope, it is possible to see that the cell is surrounded by a thin layer. This is called the **cell membrane**, and it stops the contents of the cell from escaping. The cell membrane controls the passage of materials into and out of the cell. Normally it allows small **molecules** such as water, oxygen, and carbon dioxide to pass through, but blocks the passage of large molecules such as **proteins**. These large molecules have to be moved across the membrane using special carriers.

Materials can pass across a cell membrane in different ways. Small molecules such as oxygen **diffuse** across the membrane. Diffusion is the movement of molecules from where they are in high concentration to where they are in low concentration. This means that oxygen diffuses into a cell because there is a lower concentration inside the cell than outside. Water moves across the membrane by a special diffusion process called **osmosis**. Large molecules such as proteins need to be carried

A typical animal cell is rounded in shape, surrounded by a cell membrane. This holds in the cytoplasm, which contains other structures such as the nucleus, ribosomes, and mitochondria.

cell membrane
cytoplasm
nucleus
endoplasmic reticulum
Golgi body
free ribosome
ribosome
mitochondrion
lysosome

SCIENCE PIONEERS Robert Hooke

Robert Hooke built one of the earliest microscopes using a series of lenses that he used to look at living material. He examined tiny slivers of cork and described it as being made up of lots of tiny boxes that he called cells. His work changed the way scientists viewed the structure of living things. However, it was another 168 years before scientists observed the contents of cells.

across the membrane. Carrier molecules in the membrane pick up proteins on one side of the membrane and move them into the cell. This is called active transport. Unlike diffusion and osmosis, active transport needs energy to take place.

The **cytoplasm** fills the cell. It is made up of mostly water, often about 70 percent, the rest being molecules of salts, sugars, fats, **amino acids**, and proteins. Some of the proteins are **enzymes** that the cell has made. Enzymes control the rate of chemical reactions within the cell.

The largest structure in the cell is the **nucleus**. Usually lying toward the middle of the cell, it is the most important part of the cell. The nucleus is the control center and sends out messages to other parts of the cell, controlling the production of molecules such as proteins. The ability to control production comes from the **chromosomes**, which lie within the nucleus. Chromosomes can only be seen clearly when the cell is dividing; they appear as threads within the nucleus. In human cells, there are 46 chromosomes, or 23 pairs. Chromosomes are made from **DNA (deoxyribonucleic acid)** and protein. The DNA holds the genetic code that is used to make proteins.

The difference in size between an egg (female sex cell) and a sperm (male sex cell) can be seen clearly here as the sperm cluster around the egg.

PLANT CELLS

Plant cells differ from animal cells in several ways. One obvious difference is their size: plant cells tend to be larger than animal cells. They also have a regular shape, because their cell membrane is surrounded by a cell wall that is rigid and gives the cell a fixed shape. The cell wall contains a substance called **cellulose**. Cellulose is made up of lots of long chains of **glucose**. The wall is strong but **permeable**, so gases and water can pass through. Due to their regular shape, plant cells can pack tightly together, leaving no air spaces. Some plant cells are more polygonal (five-sided) in shape, and they often have extra cellulose laid down in the corners. This provides the additional support that is needed in stems.

The main features in a plant cell include the cellulose cell wall, the large central vacuole, and chloroplasts in the cytoplasm.

cell wall

cell membrane

chloroplast

vacuole

nucleus

cytoplasm

THE VACUOLE AND SUPPORT

Plant cells have a large space in the center called a vacuole. This contains cell sap, which is a watery solution of sugar and salts. The vacuole is so large that it pushes the cytoplasm and nucleus to the side. The vacuole pushes on the contents, making the whole cell very firm. This helps to support the plant. If a plant does not get enough water, it wilts and its shoots droop. This happens because the vacuole loses water and the cells shrink slightly. This means there is less support, so the leaf or the stem loses rigidity.

THE CYTOPLASM AND PHOTOSYNTHESIS

The cytoplasm of a plant cell usually contains small particles that contain **pigments**, **starch**, or oil. These particles are called **plastids**. **Chloroplasts** contain the green pigment **chlorophyll**, and they are involved in the process of **photosynthesis**. A chloroplast is usually disc-shaped and about 5 to 8 μm in length and 2 to 4 μm wide. Cells where photosynthesis happens have between 20 and 40 chloroplasts. Cells in the root contain colorless plastids that are full of starch. The starch is used as a food store by the plant. For example, potato **tubers** contain cells that are full of starch grains.

PLANT OR ANIMAL?

The differences between plant and animal cells are shown in this table:

Plant cells	Animal cells
Cellulose cell wall outside of the cell membrane	No cell wall
Many plant cells have a regular shape	Usually irregular in shape
Many plant cells have a large vacuole filled with cell sap	Only have tiny vacuoles
Often have chloroplasts which contain chlorophyll	No chloroplasts
Some plant cells have starch grains	No starch grains

JOURNEY INTO THE CELL

The electron microscope has allowed scientists to really explore the cell. They have discovered a "cellular city" of tiny structures called **organelles**. Each type of organelle performs a particular function. For example, there are power stations (mitochondria), waste disposal stations (lysosomes), protein factories (ribosomes), and protein packaging and export facilities (the endoplasmic reticulum and Golgi body).

This diagram shows the size of different structures such as cells, organelles, bacteria, and viruses. It also shows the different sizes that are visible using either an electron microscope or a light microscope.

$1\mu m$ (micrometer) = 0.000039 inch
$1nm$ (nanometer) = 0.000000039 inch

| 0.1nm | 1nm | 10nm | 100nm | $1\mu m$ | $10\mu m$ | $100\mu m$ |

Light microscope

Electron microscope

Atoms

Lipids

Small molecules

Virus

Proteins

Chloroplasts

Most bacteria

Animal and plant cells

POWER CELLS

The mitochondria (singular: mitochondrion) are the power stations of the cells. They are the sites of **aerobic respiration** and produce nearly all the energy the cells require to function. The energy is locked up in a very useful molecule called ATP. All cells use this for energy. Mitochondria have two membranes: an inner and an outer membrane. The inner membrane is highly folded, which increases its surface area for making ATP.

TRANSPORTATION AND MAKING PROTEINS

The endoplasmic reticulum (ER) is the transportation network for the cell. It is made up of a network of tubes that criss-cross the cell. It allows substances such as protein to be moved from one part of the cell to another.

Some of the ER has tiny particles called ribosomes attached to it. Ribosomes are the protein factories where the manufacturing of protein takes place. This is called protein synthesis. Proteins are made up of lots of smaller molecules called amino acids. Amino acids are carried to the ribosomes and joined together in long chains to form proteins. Protein synthesis is extremely important to cells, so there are often hundreds or thousands of ribosomes found in cells.

MANUFACTURING AND WASTE DISPOSAL

The Golgi body looks a bit like a stack of tubes. It is responsible for making new products. For example, it makes glycoproteins from proteins and **carbohydrates**. It packages the new products into small membrane-bound sacs called vesicles, which are moved around the cell or sent outside the cell.

The lysosomes are responsible for breaking down waste materials and old organelles within the cell. A lysosome is simply a bundle of enzymes contained within a membrane. It fuses with unwanted materials and pours its enzymes over them in order to break them down. The materials from this breakdown are either recycled in the cell or sent outside.

All Sorts of Cells

There are many different types of cells in existence, each one slightly different. There are some organisms that consist of just one large cell that does everything, while complex organisms such as mammals have many different types of cells, each adapted to carry out a particular job.

SPECIALIZED CELLS

The amoeba is a single-celled organism that carries out all its functions within its one cell. In a slightly more complex animal such as a hydra or jellyfish, there are seven types of cells, each with a particular job. There are sensory cells that react to touch, stinging cells that are used by the hydra to catch and poison prey, and nerve cells that carry messages from one part of the body to another.

The hydra is an animal that has a sac-shaped body and tentacles that are covered with stinging cells.

There are also feeding cells that release chemicals to digest the food. In more complex animals, there are even more types of cell, each specialized to carry out a specific job within the body.

CELL SHAPE AND SIZE

The shapes of cells are quite varied. Plant cells are encased in a rigid wall, so they tend to be rectangular. In contrast, animal cells have a flexible cell membrane with no cell wall, so they can be many different shapes. For example, they can be incredibly long and thin like neurons (nerve cells), doughnut-shaped like red blood cells, or flat like the cells lining the inside of the mouth.

The size of cells is often related to their function. An egg cell is usually very large and is often the largest cell that an organism produces. It is packed full with food that will be used by the cell to grow once it has been fertilized. Cells involved in the uptake of materials such as oxygen or water tend to have a large surface area, and they are often flat in shape. Their surface area may be further increased by the presence of microvilli, which are tiny folds and wrinkles in the membrane.

HOW BIG CAN A CELL BE?

There is a limit to how large a cell can grow. As a cell gets larger, its volume increases, but the area of its surface membrane does not increase as much. This causes problems for the cell. A larger cell needs more oxygen and food, but the cell membrane may not have a large enough surface area for transporting materials into the cell. Also, as the cell gets larger, the middle of the cell gets farther away from the cell membrane and it takes longer for materials to be moved around the cytoplasm. This means that there is an ideal size for each particular type of cell.

NERVE CELLS

The **nervous system** is made up of cells called neurons, or nerve cells. Neurons are specialized to carry messages in the form of electrical impulses all around the nervous system. There are billions of these cells, with more than 100 billion neurons in the brain alone.

AXONS AND DENDRONS

Although neurons have a number of parts in common with all animal cells, including a cell membrane, cytoplasm, and a nucleus, their appearance is quite different from other cells. The main part of the neuron is the cell body, which contains the nucleus and most of the cytoplasm. The rest of the neuron is made up of nerve fibers. These are thin threads of cytoplasm that extend out from the cell body.

Often axons are covered with a layer of myelin, which is like insulation around electrical wire. Myelin is made of fat, and it helps to speed up the transmission of an impulse along an axon.

dendrites

dendron

nucleus

nerve ending

myelin sheath

axon

cell body

The longest nerve fiber is usually called the axon, while the shorter ones are called dendrons and dendrites. These fibers carry the electrical messages, called impulses, along the length of the cell.

The dendrites make connections with other neurons. They pick up messages and pass them to dendrons, which carry them to the cell body. Dendrites can be located on one or both ends of the neuron. From the cell body, the message travels along the axon.

Neurons are the oldest and longest cells in the body. You have many of the same neurons for your whole life. Although other cells die and are replaced, many neurons are never replaced when they die. In fact, you have fewer neurons when you are old compared to when you are young. Neurons can be quite large: a single sensory neuron from your fingertip has an axon that extends the length of your arm.

SCIENCE PIONEERS Schleiden and Schwann

Matthias Jakob Schleiden (1804–1881) and Theodor Schwann (1810–1882) carried out some of the earliest studies of cells. In 1838 Schleiden discovered that all the various parts of plants were made of cells. His research showed that the nucleus was the control center of the cell. Schwann recognized that some organisms were unicellular (single-celled), while others were multicellular (many-celled). He also discovered that the ovum (egg) was a single cell, and he observed that after **fertilization**, the egg divided repeatedly to develop into a complex organism.

SENSORY AND MOTOR NEURONS

There are several types of neuron in the body, two of which are the sensory neurons and motor neurons. The sensory neurons carry impulses from sensory receptors to the brain or spinal cord. Sensory receptors are cells that detect changes in the surroundings—for example, a pain receptor or temperature receptor in the skin. Motor neurons carry messages from the brain or spinal cord to the muscles.

A good example of how these neurons work together is the spinal reflex. A reflex is an instant reaction to something. For example, if you touch a hot object, your finger is immediately jerked away. You do not have to think about doing anything—it just happens automatically. Reflexes are designed to protect you. The reflex does not involve the brain, since it would take too long for the message to be carried all the way to the brain and back. Instead, reflex messages are carried along a simple loop that involves the sensory neurons, the motor neurons, and the spinal cord. When you touch something hot, sensory receptors in your fingertip detect the heat and a message is sent along a sensory neuron to the spinal cord. The message is then passed on to a motor neuron. This carries the message to muscles in the arm. The muscles contract, pulling the finger away from the hot object.

THE BRAIN

The human brain is a pinkish-gray mass made up of about ten billion nerve cells, all linked together. The brain is the control center for movement, sleep, hunger, thirst, and virtually every other vital process essential for our survival. The largest part of the brain is the cerebrum, which is made up of two cerebral hemispheres. **Conscious** thought and memory take place here. The different parts of the cerebrum have specific functions. For example, there are areas concerned with sight, speech, memory, and personality. The cerebellum controls the coordination of body movements, while the medulla oblongata controls the heartbeat and breathing.

The brain of an adult human weighs about 3.3 pounds (1.5 kilograms). The surface of the cerebrum is highly folded. It is split down the middle into two halves called cerebral hemispheres. These two halves are connected to each other. The cerebellum and the medulla oblongata lie beneath the cerebrum.

Did you know . . . ?

The brain is surrounded and protected by three membranes called the meninges. The two inner membranes enclose a fluid that acts as a shock-absorber to protect the brain from physical injury. The disease meningitis is caused by bacteria or viruses infecting the membranes. The membranes swell up and become inflamed. Some forms of meningitis are very serious and need to be treated quickly.

THE BLOOD

Blood is made up of a liquid called plasma, which contains three types of cell: red blood cells, white blood cells, and platelets. Each of these cells has a particular role in the body.

There are between four and six million red blood cells per cubic millimeter, but only between 5,000 and 9,000 white blood cells.

RED BLOOD CELLS

Red blood cells are the most numerous cells in the blood. Their role is to pick up oxygen in the lungs and carry it to the other cells in the body. In order to do this, they contain a protein called hemoglobin, which can pick up oxygen. Each molecule of hemoglobin can carry four molecules of oxygen. Hemoglobin is red in color, which is why red blood cells are red.

The red blood cell has a round shape, but unlike most other cells, it lacks a nucleus. The cell does not need a nucleus because it only has a short life span. The lack of a nucleus gives the cell a sunken appearance, a bit like a doughnut in that they are thinner in the middle and thicker around the edges. The absence of the nucleus provides more space for hemoglobin, while the sunken shape provides a larger surface area for picking up oxygen. Red blood cells are very flexible, with the ability to twist and bend through the narrowest blood vessels, the capillaries. Only one red blood cell can squeeze through a capillary at a time, which means that the oxygen has time to leave the red blood cell and diffuse into the cells.

Red blood cells are made in the **bone marrow**. During the formation of a red blood cell, the cell loses its nucleus and much of its cytoplasm. The life span of a red blood cell is about 120 days, during which time it circulates continuously in the bloodstream. When the red blood cells are too old and no longer function properly, they are taken to the liver, where they are broken down.

TRAINING AT HIGH ALTITUDE

When you travel high up into the mountains, the air has less oxygen, and it becomes increasingly difficult to breathe. If you spend some time in the mountains, the body compensates by making more red blood cells. If there are more red blood cells, the body can pick up more oxygen. Often athletes travel to mountainous areas to train. This altitude training boosts their red blood cell count, and when they return to sea level they still have the extra cells and can perform better in races.

Mountain climbers on the world's highest mountains get breathless easily, so they have to be very careful.

Did you know ...?

The blood in an adult human contains about 25 trillion red blood cells and has to replace them at the rate of about three million per second. Each red blood cell has about 280 million hemoglobin molecules and can pick up 1.1 billion molecules of oxygen.

CELLS FOR PROTECTION AND HEALING

WHITE BLOOD CELLS

White blood cells protect the body against disease. These cells are rounded in appearance and have a nucleus. We have far fewer white blood cells than red blood cells. A drop of blood usually contains between 5,000 to 9,000 white blood cells, although this increases greatly during times of illness. They are made in the bone marrow and have a lifespan of between thirteen and twenty days, after which time they are destroyed.

White blood cells are continually on the lookout for signs of disease. When germs like bacteria or viruses invade the body, the white blood cells have a number of ways they can attack. Some white blood cells produce substances called **antibodies**. The antibodies attach to germs and destroy them. Other types of white blood cells, called neutrophils, surround the germ and destroy it.

The neutrophil seeks out invading bacteria. When it finds one, its membrane flows around the bacteria and pulls it into the neutrophil cell, where it is digested.

If the germs persist and start to increase in number, the white blood cells multiply, too. The presence of germs in the body causes the white blood cells to release a substance that stimulates the bone marrow into producing more white blood cells. Within a couple of hours, the number of white blood cells seeking out germs can double. Once the germs have all been destroyed, the number of white blood cells soon falls back to normal. However, a consistently high number of white blood cells may be a symptom of **leukemia**, a **cancer** of the blood. A leukemia patient may have as many as 50,000 white blood cells in a single drop of blood.

PLATELETS

The body has to be able to stop blood loss quickly if a blood vessel is damaged, such as when you cut yourself. Platelets play an important part in blood clotting. When bleeding starts, platelets gather at the wound and try to block the flow of blood by forming a clot. A clot begins to form when the blood is exposed to air. The platelets sense the presence of air and break apart. This releases chemicals that stimulate the formation of tiny threads that form a weblike pattern. This pattern traps blood cells, and when it hardens, it forms a scab.

SCIENCE PIONEERS Blood tranfusions

Every day, **blood transfusions** save thousands of lives. People receive blood either during a blood transfusion or an operation. The first successful blood transfusion was performed by Richard Lower in 1666, when he transferred blood from one dog to another. The following year, he carried out a successful blood transfusion on a human using blood from a sheep.

In 1795 Philip Syng Physick carried out the first known human blood transfusion, in Philadelphia.

WHY DOES A CELL BECOME SPECIALIZED?

The process of specialization is very complex. So, how do cells change and become specialized for different jobs?

ANIMAL SPECIALIZATION

The first cells produced by an **embryo** are all the same. A fertilized egg cell divides into two identical cells, and then into four, eight, and sixteen cells, and so on. Each new cell is identical to the parent cell. The process of cell division is called **mitosis** (see page 37). However, once the embryo has about 100 cells, it enters a different stage. It starts to change shape, and the cells become different and undertake new roles. As a cell becomes specialized, it loses some structures and may gain others. For example, cells that are to become red blood cells lose their nucleus, while nerve cells develop long cytoplasmic extensions. In humans, there about 200 different cell types, all of which are derived from a single fertilized egg cell.

This ball of cells is an embryo. At this stage, all the cells are identical, and they are dividing by mitosis to make more identical cells.

Scientists study embryos at different stages of development in order to learn about the process of change. They believe that cells know how to change from their position in the embryo and from the type of cells that surround them. For example, a cell on the outside of the embryo will become a skin cell, while a cell toward the middle changes into a cell that lines the intestines. Muscle cells form from cells lying in the middle of the embryo. Chemicals may be produced that control the change, too.

This photograph of a root tip shows the area where cell division is taking place. The tip of the root is protected by a root cap. Immediately behind the root cap is an area of small cells that are dividing all the time. The new cells are pushed farther back, and as this happens they get larger and become specialized.

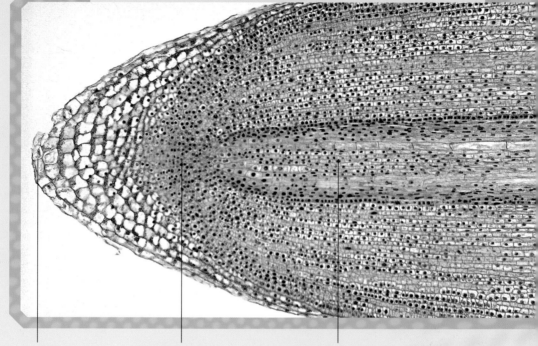

root cap   area of cell division   area of cell growth and specialization

PLANT SPECIALIZATION

Plant cells become specialized, too. New cells are only made in specific areas of a plant—for example, in the shoot and root tips and in the buds. Here, unspecialized cells divide repeatedly to form new cells. As new cells form, the older cells get pushed away. The cell becomes elongated in shape and a vacuole appears. As the cell gets farther away, it starts to become specialized in order to carry out a particular job. For example, a sieve tube cell transports sugar. It loses its nucleus, and its cytoplasm is crushed to the sides of the cell. This makes more room for moving sugar. The cell is rectangular in shape, and the cell walls at the ends of the cell have tiny pores in them, allowing sugar to move from one cell to the next.

Cells, Tissues, and Organs

Cells in multicellular organisms are not arranged haphazardly, but rather carefully organized into tissues, organs, and systems.

TISSUES, ORGANS, AND SYSTEMS

A tissue is a group of similar cells that work together to carry out a particular job—for example, muscle or nerve tissue. Tissues are grouped together into organs. An organ is a structure that contains at least two different types of tissue that work together for a common purpose. There are many different organs in the body, including your liver, kidneys, and heart. Even your skin is an organ. The stomach, for example, is an organ that contains tissues that produce digestive enzymes, muscle tissue in the stomach wall, as well as connective tissue that joins all the different tissues together.

Groups of organs work together to carry out various vital functions in the body. Such a group is called a system. For example, the digestive system includes the mouth, stomach, pancreas, and small and large intestines, while the urinary system consists of the kidneys and bladder. Other important systems in the body include the blood system, reproductive system, and respiratory (breathing) system.

MUSCLE TISSUE

Muscles are made of tissues that work by getting shorter, or contracting. This is possible because they contain fibers made up of protein. However, the process of contracting uses up a lot of energy, so their cells need a constant supply of food and oxygen, which is bought in by blood vessels.

There are three kinds of muscle tissue in the human body: striated or skeletal, smooth, and cardiac muscle. Striated muscle is attached to the bones of the skeleton, like the biceps and triceps muscles in the arm. You can control these muscles. Striated muscle is named because of the way the cells are arranged, giving it a striped appearance. This tissue is unusual since it is not visibly divided into cells along its length. Instead, there are bundles of long fibers. When these fibers contract, the whole muscle gets shorter.

Smooth muscle is found in a number of places in the body, including the wall of the intestine, stomach, and the bladder. This type of muscle can contract on its own. Unlike striated muscle, you have no control over smooth muscle. The muscle in the stomach wall contracts slowly to mix the food in the stomach, while smooth muscle in the intestines contracts to push the food along.

Cardiac muscle is found only in the heart, and it contracts and relaxes rhythmically throughout a person's life and never tires. It does not need nerves to make it contract. However, nerves from the brain to the heart can speed up or slow down the heartbeat.

muscle fiber   striated cytoplasm   nucleus

Striated muscle is used to move the bones of the body. It consists of long fibers and is well supplied with blood vesslels that bring oxygen.

Did you know ... ?

Muscles make up about 40 percent of an adult's body weight.

BONE TISSUE

The human skeleton is made up of bone and **cartilage**. You may not believe it, but bone is a living tissue and contains cells and blood vessels. The bulk of the bone is made up of a mineral called calcium phosphate. This mineral makes bone very hard and gives it its white appearance. There are also lots of collagen fibers, a type of protein that provides elasticity.

A bone is made up of a layer of compact bone tissue around the outside and a layer of spongy bone tissue beneath. Spongy tissue has lots of spaces between slivers of bone, and these

If you examine compact bone tissue under a microscope, you find that it is made up of rings of cells. The cells are embedded in a substance called the matrix, and this is made up of calcium phosphate and collagen, which give the bone its strength.

are filled with blood. The blood brings in oxygen and food for the cells in the bone tissue. Also, the spaces help to make the bone lighter. In the center is a space that is filled with bone marrow. Bone marrow is a soft tissue that has a lot of blood vessels. It is here that the red blood cells, white blood cells, and platelets are made.

LUNG TISSUE

The role of lung tissue is to assist the uptake of oxygen by red blood cells. The most important elements of the lung are tiny sacs called alveoli. The wall of the alveoli is made up of a single layer of epithelial cells. These cells are flat with a large surface area. Gases can pass easily across them. Wrapped around the outside of the alveoli are lots of tiny blood vessels called capillaries. Air is drawn into the lungs, filling all the alveoli. Oxygen in the air diffuses through the walls of the alveoli into the blood capillaries. Some of alveolar cells secrete a liquid that helps oxygen to diffuse more easily across the cells. Carbon dioxide in the blood diffuses in the opposite direction. It leaves the blood and diffuses through the wall of the alveoli into the air that is breathed out.

PREMATURE BABIES

One of the most common problems facing a premature baby is difficulty breathing. Because it has been born too early, the baby's lungs have not developed properly and do not produce enough of an important substance called surfactant. Surfactant allows the inner surface of the lungs to expand properly when the baby starts to breathe air for the first time. Today, women about to give birth to a premature baby are given medication just before delivery to help the baby breathe. Immediately after birth and several times later, the baby is treated with artificial surfactant.

SKIN: THE LARGEST ORGAN

The skin is the largest organ in the human body. Its roles are to protect the body, provide a barrier against microorganisms such as bacteria, and help control body temperature.

The skin is composed of three layers: the epidermis, dermis, and subcutaneous layer. The epidermis is the top layer of skin. It consists of cells tightly packed together, providing a barrier between the inside of the body and the outside world. This is called epithelial tissue. There are many epithelial layers, and new cells are constantly formed at the bottom, pushing the cells upward. As this happens, the cells become fat and hard and eventually die, forming a dead layer at the surface.

The skin is a complex organ that is specialized to perform several key functions.

erector muscle

hair

sweat pore

sebaceous (oil) gland

nerve endings

epidermis

dermis

hair follicle

sweat duct

capillaries

sweat gland

subcutaneous layer

Below the epidermis lies the dermis. The dermis is made up of tough connective fibers of collagen and elastin that support the skin and give it elasticity. As a person gets older, these fibers lose their elasticity, and the skin becomes loose and wrinkled.

The subcutaneous layer is beneath the dermis and consists mainly of cells that are packed full of large drops of oil. This is called adipose tissue, more commonly known as fat. Adipose tissue helps cushion the skin and provide insulation against the cold.

CASE STUDY Treating burns

Burns can be horrific injuries. Some burns just damage the epidermal tissue on the surface of the skin. The skin can repair these burns. But the most severe kind of burn is one that damages the dermis that lies under the epidermis. The skin cannot recover from these types of burns, and so doctors have to perform skin grafts. This is a process that involves taking healthy skin from one part of the body and attaching it to the skin that has been injured. If a person has suffered burns over much of the body, he or she may not have enough healthy skin left to supply a graft. Now, doctors can use an artificial skin that consists mostly of collagen fibers. The damaged skin is removed and the artificial skin is laid over the wound. The artificial skin helps the skin cells to grow new fibers. In time, new blood vessels grow into the area and a new skin forms over the damaged area.

This is artificial epidermis that will be used for a skin graft. This cutting-edge technology helps people with serious injuries, reducing the long-term physical effects of burns.

PLANT TISSUES

Just as in animals, plant tissues are groups of similar cells that carry out the same role. There are several different tissues in the leaf, including the epidermal and mesophyll tissue. There are tissues involved with the transportation of materials around the plant, as well as different tissues in the flower and root.

Most leaves have stomata in their lower epidermis. Each stoma is a gap in the epidermis, and it is surrounded by two sausage-shaped guard cells.

EPIDERMAL TISSUE

A plant's epidermal tissue forms the outermost layer and is the plant equivalent to animal skin. These cells are flat and form a protective layer. Often, they have a layer of cuticle on their outermost surface. This is a thin, waxy layer that waterproofs the leaf surface and helps to reduce the amount of water that evaporates from the leaf surface. In most leaves, there are gaps in the epidermis, especially the lower epidermis, called stomata that are between the epidermal cells. Each stoma is surrounded by two specialized cells called guard cells, which can open and close the stoma. The stomata allow gases such as carbon dioxide and oxygen to enter and leave and also allows water vapor to escape.

PACKING TISSUE

Simple packing tissue fills the spaces in the plant. The cells are rounded and very firm, a bit like balloons packed together with tiny air spaces in between. They provide support and a place to store materials. For example, packing tissue in the root is filled with starch.

VASCULAR TISSUE

Running through the plant are the vascular tissues, made up of xylem and phloem. These tissues are important because they transport water and food around the plant. They also provide essential support, especially the xylem. Xylem contains cells called xylem vessels that are hollow tubes. The walls of these cells are made of lignin, a very strong material. Lignin makes the cell wall impermeable, meaning nothing can pass through. Once a cell wall is completely filled with lignin, the contents of the cell die. This creates the hollow tube that forms the xylem vessels. Water move through these tubes. Hollow tubes are surprisingly strong, and so the xylem helps to hold the plant's stem erect. Phloem contains sieve tube cells that are adapted to carrying food materials around the plant. These cells have pores in their end walls so that food can pass from one cell to another. Sieve tubes have lost their nucleus, so there is more space for moving food.

LEAVES, STEMS, AND ROOTS

The main organs of the plant are the root, stem, and leaf.
A plant organ is made up of several different tissues working
together.

LEAVES

The leaf is very important, since it contains most of the
photosynthetic tissue that makes the food for the plant.
Leaves contain a network of veins, which are bundles of tubes
called xylem and phloem. Xylem carries water and minerals
into the leaf cells, and phloem carries sugars out to the plant.
A plant could not survive without its leaves. The leaf has a
large surface area and is usually flat. This means that gases
such as carbon dioxide do not have to travel very far to pass
from the air to the cells.

Upper epidermis: Single layer of cells, often with a thin waxy layer called a cuticle over the upper surface to reduce water loss.

Mesophyll: This is made up of two layers, the palisade mesophyll above and the spongy mesophyll below. The palisade mesophyll cells are bricklike in shape and are usually arranged in two or three rows below the upper epidermis. The spongy mesophyll is made up of rounded cells, loosely packed together with lots of large air spaces.

Lower epidermis: Single layer of cells with pores called stomata. Each stoma consists of a pair of guard cells surrounding an opening.

STEMS

The stems support the leaves of the plant. The vascular bundles of xylem and phloem are arranged in a ring in the cortex to provide more support.

Vascular bundle: These give support to the plant and transport materials around the plant in xylem and phloem tubes.

Pith: The cells at the center of the stem.

Epidermis: This is a single layer of cells that protects the stem.

Cortex: The space between the epidermis and the vascular bundles is filled with simple, rounded cells that act as packing tissue.

ROOTS

Roots are organs that perform two main jobs for the plant. First, they support the plant by anchoring it in the ground. Vascular bundles of xylem and phloem tubes are located in the center of the root to give more support. Second, roots take up water and minerals through specially shaped root hair cells. These are elongated epidermal cells. The water is taken up by the tiny root hairs and transported around the plant in the xylem tissue. The root hairs are positioned behind the root tip.

Making New Cells

Growth is one of the characteristics of life. Growth involves an increase in size, either through an increase in the number of cells or through an increase in the size of each individual cell.

WHY DO CELLS DIVIDE?

There is a limit to how large a cell can become, so in order to grow larger, an organism needs to make more cells. The new cells are produced by a cell dividing to form two cells. This process is called mitosis. In this type of cell division, the two new cells have the same number of chromosomes as the parent cell and are identical to it and to each other.

GROWTH

In multicellular animals, growth takes place all over the animal's body until the animal reaches its full size. In complex animals such as mammals, a few cells retain the ability to grow and divide. For example, cells in the skin continue to divide to provide a constant supply of new cells as old ones are lost. Cells in the bone marrow also continue to divide to produce new blood cells. All the other cell types lose their ability to divide. This means that some cell types cannot be replaced. An example of this is that when brain cells die, they are not replaced.

In plants, growth occurs in specialized areas called meristems. Cell division in these regions increases the length of the shoot and root. There is also a small area of growth located between the xylem and phloem in the vascular bundles. Cell division here makes the stem wider.

MITOSIS

In this type of cell division, one cell divides to form two identical cells. First, the nucleus divides into two, and this is followed by the rest of the cell dividing into two. As the nucleus starts to divide, the chromosomes become visible as threads within the nucleus. The DNA has been copied, so each chromosome consists of two identical threads joined together at one point. The chromosomes move to the middle of the cell, where they line up. Then, they move apart, each thread going in the opposite direction. Finally, the cytoplasm divides and the two new cells are formed. A nucleus forms in each of the new cells.

At the start of mitosis, the nuclear membrane disappears (step 1) and the spindle appears (step 2). The chromosomes move to the middle of the cell (step 3) and the two threads of each chromosome are pulled apart (step 4). These move to opposite ends of the cell. Finally, the nuclear membrane re-forms (step 5), and there are then two identical cells.

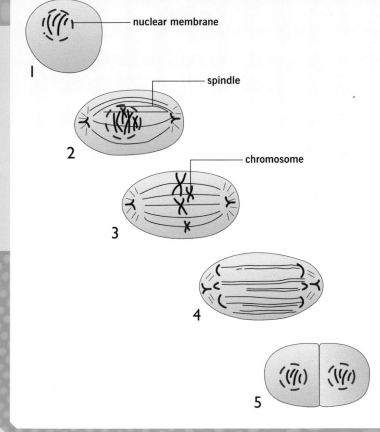

nuclear membrane

1

spindle

2

chromosome

3

4

5

REPRODUCTION

Organisms reproduce in order to produce new individuals. There are two forms of reproduction: sexual and asexual reproduction.

SEXUAL REPRODUCTION

Mammals reproduce using sexual reproduction, which involves two individuals: a male and a female. The male produces sex cells called spermatozoa that fertilize the egg cells produced by the female. The new individual is different from both of its parents.

ASEXUAL REPRODUCTION

Asexual reproduction involves a single parent and is common in single-celled organisms such as bacteria and amoebas. The parent organism reproduces simply by dividing into two. This is called binary fission. Both new cells are identical to the parent. The two new cells feed and grow, and then, if conditions are favorable, they will divide again.

A new yeast cell forms as a bud on the side of a fully grown cell. Once is it large enough, it breaks away to become an independent cell.

An amoeba may divide only once a day, whereas a bacterium may divide as much as once every twenty minutes, given the right conditions. One bacterium could become one million in just seven hours. Yeast and hydra reproduce asexually by budding. The bud grows and then separates to become an individual.

Many plants also reproduce asexually, and gardeners make use of this when they take cuttings. A cutting is simply a length of shoot removed from a plant that is placed in soil and allowed to grow roots. It grows into a new plant that is identical to the parent plant.

SCIENCE PIONEERS Walther Flemming

Zoologist Walther Flemming developed a staining technique that enabled him to watch what happened to chromosomes during cell division. The new staining techniques made it possible for Flemming to follow the process of cell division, which he named mitosis. In 1882 his results were published in the book *Cytoplasm, Nucleus and Cell Division*. It was another twenty years before the significance of Flemming's work was truly acknowledged with the rediscovery of Gregor Mendel's rules of **heredity**.

Did you know ...?

The largest and smallest cells in the human body are the **gametes**, or the sex cells. The female sex cell (egg) is about 35 μm in diameter, which is just visible to somebody with really good eyesight. The male sex cell (spermatozoon) is only about 3 μm in diameter and is the smallest cell of the human body.

CLONING

A **clone** is an individual that is genetically identical to another individual. This means that every single bit of DNA is exactly the same. Cloning is often thought of as something that only happens in a laboratory, but it can occur naturally. Identical twins are clones. They are formed when a newly fertilized egg splits into two and each part develops into a new individual. Since the twins are formed from the same cell, they are genetically identical.

Individuals that have been produced by asexual reproduction are clones, too. This includes plants that reproduce asexually. Strawberry plants produce shoots called runners that grow along the ground. New plants form at intervals along this shoot, and they are all clones of each other and of their parent plant.

IN THE LABORATORY

Recently, the term *cloning* has been associated with making copies of animals in the laboratory. The best known clone was Dolly the sheep. Normally, sheep reproduce sexually, so the offspring are different from their parents. Dolly was different: she was an identical copy of her mother.

There are two methods of laboratory cloning. One method is called embryo cloning. It is based on the natural process by which identical twins are formed. A fertilized egg is taken and, once the embryo has started to grow, the cells are pulled apart and allowed to develop into individual embryos. The offspring are clones of each other, but they are different from their parents.

The other method, called nuclear transfer, is how Dolly the sheep was created. In the first stage, scientists take an unfertilized egg and remove its nucleus. Then, a cell is taken from the animal that is to be cloned. This is called the donor cell. The nucleus is taken out of the donor cell and placed inside the empty egg. It is given a tiny burst of electricity to get it to start dividing and form a ball of cells. Then, the new embryo is implanted in the **uterus** of a female animal, where it develops until it is ready to be born.

KEY EXPERIMENT Creating Dolly

Dolly the Sheep was created by a team led by Ian Wilmut at the Roslin Institute in Scotland in the United Kingdom in 1996. Dolly's mother was a six-year-old Finn Dorset ewe (female sheep). The process was incredibly difficult, and the team experienced many failures. They tried replacing the nucleus in the egg 277 times, and they only obtained 29 embryos. All 29 embryos were placed in **surrogate** ewes, but only one survived: Dolly.

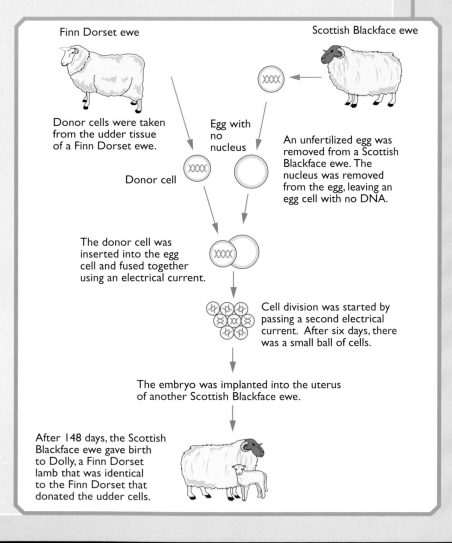

Finn Dorset ewe

Scottish Blackface ewe

Donor cells were taken from the udder tissue of a Finn Dorset ewe.

Donor cell

Egg with no nucleus

An unfertilized egg was removed from a Scottish Blackface ewe. The nucleus was removed from the egg, leaving an egg cell with no DNA.

The donor cell was inserted into the egg cell and fused together using an electrical current.

Cell division was started by passing a second electrical current. After six days, there was a small ball of cells.

The embryo was implanted into the uterus of another Scottish Blackface ewe.

After 148 days, the Scottish Blackface ewe gave birth to Dolly, a Finn Dorset lamb that was identical to the Finn Dorset that donated the udder cells.

STEM CELLS

Stem cells are special cells that retain the ability to divide, even when most other cells no longer can. When they divide, one cell remains a stem cell, but the other cell develops into a different type of cell. A stem cell in a human embryo can divide and form any one of more than 200 different types of cells. As the individual gets older, the ability to make cells decreases, and so adult stem cells can then only make a few types of cell.

MAKING AND REPLACING

The bone marrow is particularly rich in stem cells. It is here that stem cells make red blood cells, some types of white blood cell, and platelets. There are also stem cells in other organs, such as the skin and the intestines. Some tissues have stem cells that lie in wait until they are needed. If the tissue is damaged, the stem cells become active and repair the damage—for example, in muscle tissue. However, brain tissue does not have any stem cells, so it cannot make new cells, even when some die.

In the future, it may be possible to cure many diseases by growing a supply of new cells from stem cells in the laboratory. This may help people who have suffered from extensive burns, diabetes, liver disease, heart disease, and various brain disorders such as Parkinson's disease. The treatment is called cell replacement therapy. In this kind of therapy, the damaged organ or tissue is injected with cells that have been grown in the laboratory from stem cells.

STEM CELL RESEARCH AND ETHICS

Stem cells taken from embryos are the most useful to medical research, since they can be used to make a full range of cell types. They are taken from human embryos no more than fourteen days old. At this point, the embryo is the size of the period at the end of this sentence and contains about 100 cells. The cells have not started to become specialized. A few stem cells are removed and grown separately to make lots more stem cells.

The use of stem cells could offer major medical breakthroughs, but it raises many **ethical** issues that governments, scientists, and the public continue to debate. Some people believe that the use of embryonic stem cells is wrong because an embryo is a potential human life. Others believe that stem cell research, if used properly, can offer an ethical and beneficial new path in medical research. The rules governing experimentation on human embryos are very strict. Some countries have gone further and banned human stem cell research completely. However, it may be possible to avoid all these problems by taking adult stem cells from bone marrow.

The round cells in this picture are embryonic stem cells. Research that involves the use of human stem cells is controversial because it involves the destruction of a human embryo.

CELLS OUT OF CONTROL

Every minute, ten million cells divide in the human body. Normally, cell division takes place in an orderly way. But sometimes a cell goes out of control and starts to divide over and over again, creating a mass of cells called a tumor. This can sometimes lead to cancer.

CANCER

Cancer develops from a single cell that has mutated, and so the genetic material that carries the body's hereditary instructions has been changed. Instead of maturing normally and then dying, cancerous cells reproduce without control. Some divide very quickly while others divide more slowly, but they all share one feature: they never stop dividing. In fact, if a cancerous cell is removed from the body and grown in the laboratory with plenty of nutrients, it would continue to grow and divide forever.

Scientists are trying to find out what causes a cell to start dividing in an uncontrolled way. In many cases, it has been linked to chemicals in the environment called carcinogens that cause the cell to stop working normally. For example, the chemicals in cigarette smoke such as tar and nicotine may cause lung cancer by interfering with the **genes** that control normal growth in the cells of the lungs.

This picture, taken with a scanning electron microscope, shows a single breast cancer cell.

CANCER IN THE GENES

Sometimes cancers can be caused by genetic factors that are inherited. For example, some breast cancers run in families, and the women inherit certain genes from their mother that make them more likely to get breast cancer.

RECENT DEVELOPMENT Bone marrow transplants

Leukemia is the name given to a group of cancers that affect the blood. There are different forms of leukemia, and they all involve the production of abnormal white blood cells. Most cancers, including leukemia, are usually treated with **chemotherapy** and **radiation therapy**. These are treatments that target cells that divide rapidly. However, healthy stem cells in bone marrow can be damaged by these treatments, especially by high-dose chemotherapy. Without healthy bone marrow, the patient cannot make new blood cells, so patients are given a bone marrow transplant (BMT) to replace the stem cells. To minimize potential side effects, doctors use bone marrow that matches the patient's own bone marrow as closely as possible. Once patients have had their chemotherapy or radiation treatment, they receive the bone marrow from the donor.

Did you know ... ?

The word *cancer* was first used by the ancient Greek doctor Hippocrates. He thought the way tumors attached to parts of the body reminded him of crab claws, so he named the disease *karkinos*, the Greek word for crab. This word translates as *carcinoma* in English, meaning a cancerous growth.

MEIOSIS: A DIFFERENT TYPE OF DIVISION

Egg cells and spermatozoa are gametes, and they are different from all other cells in the human body. Most body cells contain 46 chromosomes, but the gametes have just 23 chromosomes. Gametes are produced from cells that contain 46 chromosomes, but the number of chromosomes in the new gamete is halved in a type of division called meiosis. Meiosis is similar to mitosis, but it involves two divisions.

During the first division, the nucleus disappears and the chromosomes become visible. The 46 chromosomes organize themselves so that they are arranged in pairs. The pairs are separated, and they move to opposite ends of the cell. Now, the rest of the cell divides. The two new cells each have 23 chromosomes. The next division starts immediately and is identical to what occurs during mitosis (see page 37). The chromosomes gather in the middle of the cell. Each of the 23 chromosomes consists of two threads, which separate and move to opposite ends of the cell. In the final step, the cell divides. By the end of meiosis, there are four cells, each of which contains 23 chromosomes.

When an egg cell with 23 chromosomes is fertilized by a spermatozoon that also has 23 chromosomes, the new embryo ends up with 46 chromosomes. If the gametes were not produced in this way, the number of chromosomes would keep on increasing.

PREGNANCY AND OLDER MOTHERS

Mistakes can happen during meiosis, causing the resulting gametes to have chromosomes that are missing parts, or there may be extra chromosomes. Older women who become pregnant are more likely to have a baby that has a chromosome defect. This is because of the age of the egg cell. The egg cells are formed in the ovary of a woman while she is still a **fetus** in her mother's uterus. Many years later, some of these egg cells may be fertilized. Due to the long period of time between the formation of the egg cell and its fertilization, there are more chances that something may go wrong.

Some babies are born with Down syndrome. They have 47 chromosomes rather than the normal 46. A baby with Down syndrome has a different appearance and may have learning difficulties. An older mother is often offered a test for abnormalities such as Down syndrome when she is about fifteen to twenty weeks pregnant. This is called an amniocentesis test. A needle is inserted through the wall of the uterus, and cells from the baby are extracted. These cells are examined under a microscope for abnormalities.

Meiosis takes place in plants, too. Flowers contain male and female parts: the anthers and carpels. Inside the anthers, meiosis takes place to produce pollen. The small pink dots in this picture are pollen cells inside the pollen sacs. You can see their nuclei colored in red.

pollen cell

pollen sac

Bacteria

Bacteria are tiny, single-celled organisms that are found everywhere, from hot pools of mud to the polar ice caps. There are lots of them, too—several million are probably living in your mouth at this very moment. They feed on a vast range of materials, from sugar and starch to sulfur and iron. Some are extremely tough, like the bacteria called *Deinococcus radiodurans*, which can withstand blasts of radiation 3,000 times greater than would kill a human being.

BACTERIAL CELLS

A bacterial cell is much simpler than a human cell. It consists of just an outer membrane and the cytoplasm. It doesn't even have a nucleus. At the center of the cell is a ball of DNA. If this DNA were stretched out into a single long strand, it would be about 1,000 times longer than the bacterial cell itself.

Often there is a capsule around the outer membrane of a bacterium to give additional protection and prevent it from drying out.

During the 1960s, bacteria were found in the hot springs of Yellowstone National Park. These bacteria can survive very high temperatures and have been studied in the laboratory for many years.

Some bacteria have long threadlike tails, called flagella, attached to the outside of the cell. They use them to move around. Bacteria can reproduce by binary fission. If provided with plenty of food and space, they can divide once every twenty minutes.

Capsule
Cell wall
Cell membrane
DNA
Cytoplasm
Flagellum

A bacterial cell has a cell wall and a cell membrane, but unlike a human cell, the DNA lies in the cytoplasm rather than in a nucleus.

SIZE AND SHAPE

Bacteria are too small to be seen with the eye and have to be examined using a light microscope. For example, the bacterium *Escherichia coli* is about 1 to 2 micrometers long, or about one-hundredth the size of a human cell.

Bacteria have distinctive shapes, and this is one of the ways by which they are identified. Spherical bacteria are called cocci. They can occur singularly, in pairs, or in chains. For example, *Streptococcus*, the bacterium that causes sore throats, forms long chains. Rod-shaped bacteria are called bacilli, and they include *E. coli* and *Salmonella*. The bacterium that causes cholera, *Vibro cholerae*, has a shape that resembles a bent rod.

SURVIVAL

Many bacteria can survive extreme environmental conditions, such as drought or freezing temperatures. They do this by forming a protective coat around themselves and becoming spores. They remain as spores until the conditions become more favorable. Then, the coat splits and the bacterium can become active again. Some bacteria can survive 50 years or more in this condition.

GENETIC ENGINEERING

Bacteria, yeast, and molds (types of fungus) make useful products, including proteins, food such as yogurt, and chemicals such as alcohol. To obtain these products, the bacteria or yeast are grown in large quantities in vats, and the product is then extracted and purified. One important product is the **antibiotic** penicillin, which is made from the mold called *Penicillium*.

MAKING LIFE EASIER

With new developments in genetic engineering, it is now possible to change the DNA of organisms such as bacteria so that they can make something that they would not normally produce. One such product is insulin. Insulin controls the level of glucose (a sugar) in the blood. However, people who suffer from diabetes are unable to produce enough insulin, and they cannot control their blood glucose levels. If untreated, this can cause serious medical problems, such as heart disease, kidney damage, and blindness. People with diabetes have to be given injections of insulin to help them control their glucose levels. In the past, the insulin came from other mammals, and this caused side affects. Now, bacteria have been altered so that they can make human insulin. This doesn't cause so many side effects and has helped many sufferers of diabetes.

One product of a genetically modified yeast is used in cheese making. Traditionally, cheese is made by mixing milk with a substance called rennet—which causes the milk to separate into solids called curds—and with a liquid called whey. The curds are removed, pressed into shape, and become cheese. Rennet contains enzymes that are obtained from the stomach of calves after they have been slaughtered. Many vegetarians do not like the idea of eating cheese that contains this animal product. Now, there is an alternative to rennet called chymosin, which is obtained from genetically altered yeast cells.

Genetic engineering is incredibly useful. There are many other examples of how genetic engineering can help us, including new **vaccines** for the disease hepatitis, which damages the liver. They can also be used in the creation of human growth **hormones**. Human growth hormones are given to children who are not growing properly and are much shorter than normal. Previously this hormone could only be obtained from the bodies of people who had died and was incredibly expensive, and so very few people could be treated. Now, bacteria have been altered to make this hormone, and so it is easier to obtain.

This is a fermentation unit (bioreactor) that uses genetically modified bacteria to produce proteins for medicine.

Did you know ... ?

Bacteria live on or in just about every material and environment on Earth. Each square inch of your skin has on average 32 million bacteria living on it. A single teaspoon of topsoil contains more than a billion bacteria.

BACTERIA AND DISEASE

Bacteria are responsible for many of the diseases that affect people. They get into the body through the mouth, nose, or cuts to the skin. Once inside the body, they attack the cells. Some stick to the outside of cells and damage them. Other bacteria produce toxins or poisons that harm the body. For example, *Salmonella* bacteria, which cause food poisoning, release a toxin that passes into the blood stream and causes diarrhea and fever.

Once bacteria are in the body, they start to multiply very quickly. The time between infection and showing signs of the disease is called the incubation period. This may be a few hours, several days, or even weeks, depending on the type of bacteria.

It is easy for bacteria to spread when an infected person sneezes in a crowded place.

SPREADING DISEASE

Many bacterial diseases are contagious, which means the bacteria spread from person to person. Bacteria can be spread through droplets in the air. When an infected person sneezes, millions of bacteria are shot into the air and may be inhaled by another person. Colds and flu are spread in this way. Bacteria may infect drinking water or food. Cholera is a major health threat after natural disasters such as earthquakes or flooding, because sewage gets washed into rivers and this water is then used for drinking, bathing, and cleaning food utensils. Animals may carry bacteria—for example, the bacteria that cause plague are carried by rat fleas.

Each year millions of people die from bacterial diseases. The biggest killer is tuberculosis (TB), a disease that affects the lungs. It kills as many as three million people every year. A major cause of death of young children in the developing world is diarrhea, a disease caused by a range of organisms, including bacteria. The bacteria are spread in contaminated water. Diarrhea results in the body losing a lot of water and the child becoming dehydrated. It is treated using rehydration salts.

SCIENCE PIONEERS Robert Koch

One of the most important bacteriologists at the end of the 19th century was the German Robert Koch. He spent a lot of time studying bacteria under a microscope. Koch established that a number of diseases were caused by bacteria. He took blood samples from people who had a particular disease and allowed bacteria from the blood to grow. Then, he injected the bacteria into mice and found that the mice got the same disease. In 1905 he received the Nobel Prize in Physiology or Medicine for his work in developing a test for tuberculosis.

ANTIBIOTICS

One way to fight a bacterial disease is to use antibiotics, which are chemicals that kill bacteria. The very first antibiotic was penicillin. Now, there are many types of antibiotics, which all work in different ways. Some attack the bacterial cell wall, making it weaker and allowing the contents of the cell to leak out. Some act by slowing down bacterial growth. Others cause the bacteria to clump together, so that they are more easily destroyed by white blood cells.

Bacteria are growing on the surface of the nutrient agar jelly. The discs have been soaked in an antibiotic that spreads out from the disc. The antibiotic has stopped the growth of bacteria, as seen by the clear area around the discs.

PROTECTING AGAINST BACTERIA

The body protects itself naturally by building up immunity against a disease. If you suffer from an illness, white blood cells increase in number. Some of the white blood cells seek out the bacteria and kill them. Other types of white blood cell produce chemicals called antibodies. Antibodies attach themselves to invading bacteria and destroy them. There are a lot of different antibodies, and each one works against a different type of bacteria. Sometimes it takes a while to make enough of the right antibodies, and the bacteria have a chance to breed and increase in number. This causes the symptoms of the disease to appear. Eventually the antibodies overcome the bacteria and the person recovers. However, the next time that type of bacteria invades, the body recognizes it immediately. Lots of antibodies are made quickly, so the bacteria are destroyed before they can cause the disease. The person has become immune to the disease.

Today, children are **vaccinated** against many diseases. A vaccine contains either a dead or weakened version of the bacterium or virus. This is injected, and the body reacts by producing lots of antibodies. You don't get the disease because the organisms have been weakened or killed. But the next time this organism invades your body, antibodies are produced quickly and the organism is killed. Sometimes a single vaccination is sufficient to protect you for life, but often a second vaccination is needed. Booster vaccinations may be given every few years as protection wears off.

SCIENCE PIONEERS Alexander Fleming

Alexander Fleming was the first to discover substances that could kill bacteria. In 1928 he was growing bacteria in the laboratory and just by chance noticed that a mold had killed some of the bacteria. He identified the mold as *Penicillium*. It took twelve years before the substance produced by the *Penicillium* could be extracted and used medically. The new miracle drug was called penicillin.

SUPERBUGS

Bacteria reproduce quickly. If a change occurs in their DNA, the change is soon passed on to new generations of bacteria. Some of these changes make the bacteria more **resistant** to drugs such as antibiotics. Antibiotics are the main weapon against bacteria, but they have been overused. Now, many types of bacteria are resistant to them.

A big problems in hospitals at the moment is the rise of the so-called superbug MRSA (methicillin resistant *Staphylococcus aureus*). This bacterium has become resistant to commonly used antibiotics. These bacteria are commonly found on the skin and in the throat and do not cause too many problems for healthy people. However, they can cause severe infections in sick or weak patients in the hospital, since the bacteria can enter their body through a burn, wound, or surgical scar. Antibiotics can be used to combat the infection, but powerful doses are required and fewer and fewer antibiotics are effective. The best way to fight these bacteria is good hygiene—for example, washing hands before touching a patient and making sure the hospital is clean.

The spread of bacteria in hospitals can be reduced by the use of clean protective clothing, such as gowns and face masks, and the cleaning of hands with antibacterial soap.

Maxx | Brush

CASE STUDY Viruses

Most people get a cold or flu at some point in their lives. These diseases, and many others, are caused by viruses. Viruses are extremely small, usually a thousand times smaller than a bacterium: just 17 to 300 nm in length. They can only be observed using an electron microscope. A virus particle consists of a protein coat wrapped around a strand of DNA or **RNA**.

Viruses do not have a cell membrane or even a nucleus or cytoplasm. They are nothing like other organisms. In fact, most of the time, they exist as inactive particles that are hardly living. Viruses need to reproduce, but they do not have the machinery to build new particles themselves, so they invade a cell and instruct it how to make new viral particles. The cell that they invade is called the host, and each type of virus has its own preferred type of cell to infect.

This is a virus viewed through an electron microscope.

The viral particle attaches to the outside of its host cell and injects its DNA or RNA into the cell. Once inside, the viral DNA or RNA takes over the operation of the cell, directing the cell to make more viral particles. Eventually the cell is so full of new viral particles that it bursts open, freeing the particles to attack new cells. Using this system, the virus can reproduce and infect other cells at an amazing rate. Antibiotics have no effect on a virus because a virus is not alive. There is nothing to kill! The best way to fight viral diseases is **immunization**.

Future Cells

In recent years, scientists have been able to discover more about the structure of the cell using the latest electron microscopes. In the future, it is likely that most of the new research will focus on how cells can be controlled or altered— for example, how stem cells can be used to treat human disease and how bacterial cells can be altered to make new products.

NEW SOURCES OF STEM CELLS

Ethical concerns about the use of human embryos in stem cell research continue to be debated. However, some scientists are avoiding this problem by taking stem cells from the umbilical cord that links a baby to its mother's placenta. A new source of stem cells is important as more and more uses are being proposed for stem cells.

Other researchers have found a way of treating bone marrow stem cells so that they are more likely to develop into brain cells after they are injected into the brain. This may lead to treatments of diseases such as Alzheimer's disease.

Another possible alternative to using embryonic stem cells may be a method that tricks human egg cells into dividing, even though they have not been fertilized. These "embryos" contain just the chromosomes from the mother and so cannot develop into babies. The tricked eggs are allowed to divide for four or five days, until they reach 50 to 100 cells. However, research is at the early stage, and no one is sure that stem cells produced in this way will behave normally.

MAKING NEW ORGANS

Researchers are working to find ways to make new organs for transplant operations in the laboratory, thus avoiding the need to take organs from people who have just died. One of the first organs made in the laboratory was a dog's bladder. The bladder was transplanted into a dog, where it worked for the next eleven months. It may be possible to use similar methods to make human organs in the future.

CLEANING UP THE ENVIRONMENT

Around the world, there are areas of industrial land with soil contaminated by toxic chemicals. The land cannot be reused until the soil is treated. One way to solve the problem is to remove the soil, but that would create a large quantity of waste that would need to be burned or buried elsewhere. A better way would be to treat the soil where it is. This may be possible using bacteria that have been modified just for this purpose.

This human ear was grown on the back of a mouse in the laboratory. A plastic scaffold was inserted together with human cartilage cells. Once formed, the ear was removed from the mouse without killing it.

Further Resources

MORE BOOKS TO READ

The DK Nature Encyclopedia. New York: Dorling Kindersley, 1998.

Stockley, Corinne. *The Usborne Illustrated Dictionary of Biology*. Tulsa, Okla.: EDC, 2000.

Tesar, Jenny E. *Stem Cells*. San Diego, Calif.: Blackbirch Press, 2003.

Viegas, Jennifer. *Cell Functions: Understanding How Cells Work*. New York: Rosen, 2005.

USING THE INTERNET

Explore the Internet to find out more about cells and cell function. You can use a search engine, such as www.yahooligans.com or www.google.com, and type in keywords such as *cell membrane*, *genetic engineering*, *mitosis*, or *stem cells*.

These search tips will help you find useful websites more quickly:

- Know exactly what you want to find out about first.
- Use only a few important keywords in a search, putting the most relevant words first.
- Be precise. Only use names of people, places, or things.

Disclaimer

All the Internet addresses (URLs) given in this book were valid at the time of going to press. However, due to the dynamic nature of the Internet, some addresses may have changed, or sites may have ceased to exist since publication. While the author and publishers regret any inconvenience this may cause readers, no responsibility for any such changes can be accepted by either the author or the publishers.

Glossary

adapt change to suit a particular habitat or environment

aerobic respiration chemical process that takes place in a cell to release energy from sugar, using oxygen

agar jelly gel made from seaweeds

amino acid building block of proteins

antibiotic substance that kills or inhibits the growth of bacteria

antibody special protein made by white blood cells that attaches to any foreign cells and inactivates them

bacteria single-celled organism that has no nucleus. Bacterial DNA is contained freely in the cytoplasm.

blood transfusion transfer of blood from one person to another

bone marrow liquidlike tissue found in the center of the body's largest bones. Bone marrow is a source of stem cells and makes red blood cells, some white blood cells, and platelets.

cancer disease caused by the uncontrollable growth of cells

carbohydrate chemical, such as sugar or starch, that contains carbon, hydrogen, and oxygen

cartilage flexible tissue that is found at the surfaces at joints in the skeleton. It also forms structures such as the ear.

cell membrane outer boundary of a cell that surrounds the cytoplasm and controls the movements of molecules into and out of the cell

cellulose substance found in the cell walls of plants, it is made of lots of units of sugars joined together in chains

chemotherapy treatment of cancer using chemicals to kill the cancerous cells

chlorophyll chemical used by plants to capture the Sun's energy

chloroplast structure in the plant cell that contains chlorophyll

chromosome threadlike structure found within the nucleus of cells

clone genetically identical copy

cloning making clones

conscious having an awareness of the surroundings and having sensations and thoughts

cytoplasm jellylike substance that fills the cell. The components of the cell are suspended in it.

diffuse   movement of molecules from an area where they are in high amounts to one where they are in low amounts

DNA (deoxyribose nucleic acid)   molecule that carries the genetic code. It is found in the nucleus of the cell.

electron   tiny negatively charged particles that travel around the nucleus of an atom

embryo   fertilized egg in its early stages of development

enzyme   protein molecule that changes the rate of chemical reactions in living things without being affected itself in the process

ethical   relating to the issue of right and wrong

fertilization   joining together of a male and female sex cell

fetus   unborn baby more than eight weeks into development

focus   cause light rays to converge (meet) on a point

fungi   organisms that are neither plants nor animals. They do not move around and cannot photosynthesize.

gamete   sex cell

genetic engineering   field of technology that involves the manipulation of genetic information

gene   unit of inheritance passed on from parent to offspring

glucose   type of sugar

heredity   handing down of genes form parent to offspring

hormone   chemical message in the body, it is carried in the blood

immunization   process by which a person becomes immune to a disease. Immunization is often carried out by injection of a vaccine.

lens   something that focuses rays of light into a sharp image

leukemia   cancer that affects the white blood cells

mitosis   type of cell divison where each cell splits to create two identical cells

molecule   group of atoms bonded together

nervous system   system including the brain, spinal cord, and nerves that controls the body's responses to things

nucleus   central part of the cell, it contains the DNA

organ   part in the body made up of different tissues, carrying out a particular function

organelle   specialized structure within a living cell

organism   individual living thing, such as a plant or animal

osmosis   special type of diffusion that involves the membrane, which is only permeable (allowing passage) to certain molecules

permeable   allowing the passage of something—for example, water or gases

photosynthesis　process by which green plants make food from carbon dioxide and water, using energy from the Sun

pigment　substance that produces a characteristic color

plastid　small organelle, found in the cytoplasm of a plant cell, that contains pigment or food

protein　large molecule made from a chain of lots of smaller molecules, called amino acids, joined together

radiation therapy　process by which high-energy radiation from X-rays and other sources are used to kill cancer cells and shrink tumors

resistant　ability of disease-causing organisms to overcome the effect of drugs such as antibiotics

RNA (ribose nucleic acid)　single stranded molecule, found in the nucleus and cytoplasm, that is involved in the production of proteins

starch　carbohydrate made by plants, it is made up of many glucose molecules joined together in a chain

stem cell　cell that retains the ability to divide and multiply and to create other types of cell

surrogate　female animal that gives birth to another female's baby

tissue　specialized cells grouped together to carry out a function

tuber　undergound stem of a plant

uterus　part of the female reproductive system in which the unborn child grows and develops

vaccinate　to inject a vaccine

vaccine　substance that usually contains weakened or dead bacteria or viruses, it is injected to bring out an immune response

virus　tiny particle usually made up of DNA or RNA coated in protein. Viruses multiply by infecting other cells.

Index